Edward Thring

Uppingham School Songs and Borth Lyrics

Edward Thring

Uppingham School Songs and Borth Lyrics

ISBN/EAN: 9783744775540

Printed in Europe, USA, Canada, Australia, Japan

Cover: Foto ©Paul-Georg Meister /pixelio.de

More available books at **www.hansebooks.com**

Edward Thring

Uppingham School Songs and Borth Lyrics

ISBN/EAN: 9783744775540

Printed in Europe, USA, Canada, Australia, Japan

Cover: Foto ©Paul-Georg Meister /pixelio.de

More available books at **www.hansebooks.com**

Uppingham School Songs

AND

Borth Lyrics

BY

EDWARD THRING

Headmaster of Uppingham School, 1853-1887

London

T. FISHER UNWIN

26, PATERNOSTER SQUARE

MDCCCLXXXVII

THIS VOLUME OF VERSE IS DEDICATED

BY THE AUTHOR'S WISH

TO

𝔄𝔫𝔫𝔞 ℭ. 𝔈. 𝔍. 𝔎𝔬𝔠𝔥

WHO THROUGH ALL HIS UPPINGHAM DAYS

MINISTERED TO HIM WITH A SISTER'S LOVE

PREFACE.

My Father had long wished to put out some work of his, which should be specially for the Boys of the School, past and present. It was suggested to him by a friend, that nothing could be better for this purpose than the School Songs, Borth Lyrics, and his other Poems, published in a small edition which all could buy, and which could be carried in a pocket. He took up the idea with great eagerness, and promised it should be his next work. The task of selecting and arranging them occupied him during his last summer holidays, spent at Birnam, in Perthshire, and he took the greatest trouble, that down to the smallest detail they should be fitting for the purpose for which he designed them. He desired to add to them, as a companion volume, the Addresses, which give some of his ideas on Teaching and Life-work. He sent his manuscripts to the publisher the day before he fell ill, having hastened their completion, as he was particularly anxious they should appear before the end of Term.

Knowing his great wish, I took up the task at once, and by the help of friends have been enabled to complete it in time.

SARAH E. THRING.

The Schoolhouse,
    UPPINGHAM.

CONTENTS.

School Songs.

	PAGE
THE UPPINGHAM SCHOOL SONG	13
FOOTBALL SONG	18
UPPINGHAM CRICKET SONG	21
THE OLD BOYS' MATCH	26
FIVES SONG	28
ECHOES OF UPPINGHAM	30
FAREWELL!	33

Borth Lyrics.

THE PROLOGUE	37
THE SUMMONS	39
THOUGHTS	41

	PAGE
The Journey	42
The Sea.—Safety	45
The Colony	47
Ripples	51
The Lery	54
The Sands	58
The Marsh Circle	62
Shells	66
Sunday.—The Hill-Top	71
The Return	74
The Flags	77

School Songs.

School Songs.

THE UPPINGHAM SCHOOL SONG.

1873.

Ho, boys, ho!
Gather round, together stand,
Raise a watchword in the land;
Stand, my merry craftsmen bold,
Brothers of the crown of gold,
Wrought in stirring days of old,
  England's crown.
Gold of hearts that know no lie,
Gold of work that does not die.
Ho, my merry craftsmen bold,
Work again the crown of gold;

Work it new, boys, young and old,
Gather, gather, near and far.
    Uppingham, hurrah, hurrah!

    Ho, boys, ho!
Here are jewels, frolic fun,
Sparkles caught from childhood's sun,
Sweetest dreams, by fancy bred,
When the dreamer's pillowed head
On his τύπτω all unsaid
    Rests and dreams.
Bring your cricket, weld it in,
Football's fire and patient shin,
Ho, my merry craftsmen bold,
Work again the crown of gold,
Work it new, boys, young and old,
Clear it rings, no flaw, nor jar.
    Uppingham, hurrah, hurrah!

Ho, boys, ho !
Bring your prizes, all your power,
Proudest aims, and gentlest hour ;
Bring the battles lost, and then
Foughten o'er and o'er again,
Till ye wrestle strength from pain.
Bring all, bring
Hopes deep down that silent lie,
Madcap schemes and purpose high ;
Ho, my merry craftsmen bold,
Work again the crown of gold
That your fathers worked of old ;
Clear it rings, each golden bar,
Uppingham, hurrah, hurrah !

Ho, boys, ho !
Fling your banner broad, each fold
Rich with heirlooms that we hold ;

Honour, lent us as a loan,
Fields of thought, by others sown,
Walls of greatness not our own,
 Where old Time
In his belfry sits, and rings
News of far-off holy things.
Memories of old, old days,
Sacred melodies of praise
Swell triumphant, as we raise
Watchword true in peace or war,
 Uppingham, hurrah, hurrah!

 Ho, boys, ho!
Gather'd in from many a land,
Foot to foot, and hand in hand.
Ho! the frolic and the fun;
Jokes that round the circle run,
Merry greetings, games we won,
 Games we lost.

New boys coming, shortly roll'd
Out of new boys into old,
Champions of the crown of gold,
Jolly hearts that grow not cold,
Hand in hand together hold,
Singing, wheresoe'er we are:

    Uppingham, hurrah! hurrah!

FOOTBALL SONG.

1866.

CROSS-LEGGED in a cave unblest,
Pitch-bedaubed, far in the West,
Wizards three themselves addrest
To a charm of wild unrest.
Wax from murd'red owners rive,
Sulphur-smothered all alive,
Strip of hide of maddened bull,
Breath of cobbler, fill it full,
Point of brad-awl, keen and fine,
Needles sharp, and hempen twine,
Stitch it well within, without,
Nimble be the charm and stout.

Lively be as prick of awl,

Quick as needle, round as ball,

Tight as hemp together pull,

Light as breath, and tough as bull.

Hide it close, then let it loose,

Led by quill of watchful goose,

On a day when on the plain

Toes twice sixty sport amain.

See the madness surge and rise,

Toes twice sixty kick the skies.

Shrieks of triumph, shrieks of woe,

Heads like nuts together go.

Cowards staring, cracking shins,

Rubbing hands, and no one wins.

Heels are flying into air,

Heads and shoulders anywhere.

Now the charm is working free,

Brad-awl point and mad-bull glee.

Potent as the golden ball

Atè cast amongst them all
Banqueting in Peleus' hall,
Many a god and goddess tall,
Kicking out in sudden brawl;
Went the ugly to the wall.
Stitch it well within, without,
Nimble be the charm and stout.
Lively be as prick of awl,
Quick as needle, round as ball,
Tight as hemp together pull,
Light as breath, and tough as bull.

UPPINGHAM CRICKET SONG.

1856.

THE wickets are set,
The field is met,
Oh the royal game and free,
The school shall win,
Short out, long in,
'Tis a goodly companie.
Merry England, merry England,
Let foes say what they will,
Whilst Cricket we play
Each Summer day,
'Tis merry England still.

From field and hall,
Each yeoman tall,
And under the greenwood tree,
From tower and town,
White hand and brown,
Have won that name for me.
Merry England, merry England,
Our fathers' place we fill,
Whilst Cricket we play
Each Summer day,
'Tis merry England still.

The wickets are set,
The field is met,
Oh, who shall beat us?—who?
Our champions stand,
Now good right hand,
And wary eye be true.

Merry England, merry England,
Our fathers' place we fill,
    Whilst Cricket we play
    Each Summer day,
'Tis merry England still.

    Cricketers all,
    If wickets fall,
As fall full well they may,
    Give honour due,
    Good hearts and true,
To those who win the day.
Merry England, merry England,
Fair field and win who will,
    Whilst Cricket we play
    Each Summer day,
'Tis merry England still.

'Tis merry in hall
When beards wag all,
Let the game be lost or won,
For friend and foe
No difference know,
When the stubborn day is done.
Merry England, merry England,
Fair field and win who will,
Whilst Cricket we play
Each Summer day,
'Tis merry England still.

Our champions stand,
In many a land
They'll prove old England's fame,
In fight, each son,
Or lost, or won,
Bears high his father's name.

Merry England, merry England,
Let foes say what they will,
    For gentle and brave,
    On field and wave,
We will uphold thee still.

THE OLD BOYS' MATCH.

1862.

Summer, ho! we sought him, found him,
    Made the jolly traitor yield,
June, he caught him, caught him, bound him,
All his posies tumbled round him,
    Flung him on the cricket field.

Jolly sun, we do implore thee,
    Stay with us the whole year round,
Young boys almost do adore thee,
Old boys come to bask before thee,
    Lie still on the cricket ground.

Sunshine for the match of matches,
    All the ground a sunny shield,
Sunny hours in sunny snatches,
Sunny hits, and sunny catches,
    Sunshine on the cricket field.

Sunshine for the old who meet us,
    Old and young, a sunny game;
Sunny game, they shall not beat us,
Sunny game, though they defeat us,
    Sunny life for Uppingham.

FIVES SONG.

1856.

Oh the spirit in the ball
Dancing round about the wall,
In your eye and out again
Ere there's time to feel the pain,
Hands and fingers all alive,
Doing duty each for five.
Oh the spirit in the ball,
Dancing round about the wall!

See again, now up it goes,
Whizzing by that startled nose,
Hands and feet are everywhere,
Twinkling in the middle air,

Bodies, bodies are no more,
All is hit, and spring, and score.
Oh the spirit in the ball,
Dancing round about the wall!

Poets sung it long ago,
All the fight and all the woe,
Geryon and thundering Zeus,
Hundred-fisted Briareus,
Argus with his million eyes,
Oh, 'twas but a game of Fives.
Oh the lordly game of Fives.
Oh the spirit in the ball,
Dancing round about the wall!

ECHOES OF UPPINGHAM.

1856.

Ring out old Bells of Uppingham,
 Ring out, ring out.
How have you caught the life, the glow
Of hearts, and boyhood's eddying flow,
 To clash it forth,
With music and a shout,
In tumbling waves of sound,
 All down and round.

Ring out old Bells of Uppingham,
 Go forth, old Bells,
O'er ancient School and gables grey,
Through wreathèd nooks and flowery spray;
 Each flower, each wreath,

A young boy's hope—ah, well—
Each lichen clinging there,
    Old memories fair.

Ring out old Bells of Uppingham,
    In changeful swells.
Ring, freighted full with smiles and tears,
The hoard of thrice a hundred years,
    All boyhood's heart,
Jests, sorrows, hopes, and knells,
With Taylor's holy lore [1]
    Sweet as of yore.

Ring out old Bells of Uppingham,
    Roll down the vale,
'Twixt these low hills, o'er pleasant grass,
Round feeding sheep, by ash trees pass,
    Pass down the vale,

[1] Bishop Jeremy Taylor, Rector of Uppingham, A.D. 1642.

Steal with the Welland on
By hamlet, tower, and lea,
    Lost in the sea.

Ring out old Bells of Uppingham,
    We'll go with you,
A breathing charm o'er dale and hill,
A voice for every good and ill,
    To brethren true,
From some old church at last
A voice still rolling on,
    When we are gone.

FAREWELL!

1875.

FAREWELL, the nevermore has come,
    The nevermore
In boyhood's fairy land, I ween,
With Fancy, boyhood's fairy queen,
    On life's great shore
To stand, and work, and dream.
  Hark, hark, the old school bell
  Now rings your knell.

Then welcome bolder life, wide air,
    And larger scope.
A bonny welcome, bonny world,
And bonny light on sails unfurled,
    O welcome Hope.

Then go, then go, the while
   Our voices meet and swell
   In blithe farewell.

Farewell, and yet, where'er you go,
      We breathe a spell.
A thousand sprites at our command
'Twixt you and us from fairy land
      Brook no farewell.
The good old days live on,
   They shall not be forgot,
   Shall not, shall not.

Borth Lyrics.

Borth Lyrics.

I.

THE PROLOGUE.

O swallow, with resistless wing, that hold'st the air in fee,
O swallow, with thy joyous sweep o'er earth and sunlit sea,
O swallow, who, if night were thine, would'st wheel amongst the stars,
    Why linger round the eaves?
Unhappy! free of all the world hast knit thy soul to clay?
And glued thy heart up on the wall, thou swiftest child of day?

Claim, glorious wing, thy heritage; break, break thy prison bars,
>Nor linger round the caves.

Sweep, glorious wings, adown the wind; fly, swallow, to the west;
Before thee, life and liberty; behind, a ruined nest.
Blow, freshening breeze, sweep, rapid wing, for all the winds are thine,
>The nest is only clay.
The rapid wings were stretched in flight, the swallow sped away,
And left its nest beneath the eaves, the much-loved bit of clay,
Turned with the sun, to go where'er the happy sun might shine,
>And passed into the day.

II.

THE SUMMONS.[1]

A THOUSAND year is nought to prayer,
  One day, so God it will:
So the chapel fair, in God's clear air,
  Looks calmly from its hill;

And true and bold the schoolhouse old
  Before it sentinel,
With close at hand a trusty band
  Of comrades guards it well.

[1] School Song. (Three weeks after the return of the School in January, 1876, the fever broke out a second time. No course remained but to go. On Friday, March 14th, the boys were sent home, to meet again in three weeks at some place not yet decided upon. Thus the School at Uppingham came to an end.)

Each morn they meet, the young, young feet,
  They lightly come and go,
A changeful stream, that still doth seem
  The same, and still doth flow.

The stream shall run while shines the sun,
  And still the buttressed stone
Shall hear the beat of young, young feet,
  And count them all its own.

The fair sun shone, but ghastly and wan
  There came a spectral dream;
The stone stood fast, but a dim fear passed
  Through buttress, and roof, and beam:

With sad, sad heart life did depart,
  A ghostly silence fell;
With sad, sad heart they turned to depart,
  And—farewell, home, farewell.

III.

THOUGHTS.

DARKEST clouds drop tender rain,
Every leaf and blade is fain
Its own jewel to obtain
From the casket of its pain.

And the thunder, black as night,
Down descends in orbs of white,
For the sun to fill with light,
Tiny chambers of his might.

Precious beads of hope are pearled
On each sorrow through the world;
Softest dews of peace in showers
Lie beneath the clouded hours.

IV.

THE JOURNEY.

The ice grips cold, as cold as death,
    Yet runs the stream below;
The very spring breathes bitter breath,
    But still the flowerets blow.
Nor shall it perish from the land,
    The living seed they bore,
As forth they fared, that pilgrim band,
    As pilgrims went of yore.

Lead, river, down the mountain glen,
    Glide 'mid the sunny slopes;
Now lose thyself, now come again,
    E'en like a pilgrim's hopes.

And careless rivulets with their peace
    Smiled on the passers-by,
From many a valley, where the trees
    See but their own dear sky.

So swept they on a great bright plain,
    A charmèd breadth out-laid,
Where mountains rounded to the main
    A charmèd circle made;
And northward couched a huge hill dream,
    Which ofttimes, as it lay,
To heave and pant in sleep did seem,
    Beneath the sultry day.

And leaning up against the hill,
    Whose headland, purple-black,
The southern waters, as they fill,
    Kiss daily, and fall back,

A simple hamlet, nowise planned,
    Puts out a long arm white,
Where level sea and level sand
    Scarce know each other's right.

The mountains rule the east, but all
    The west, the sea, the sea;
Save when the sun at evenfall
    Disputes her sovereignty.
A kindly people held the land,
    A kindly race and free;
So rest they found, that pilgrim band,
    At Borth beside the sea.

V.

THE SEA.—SAFETY.

BRIGHT sea, in thy waters rolled
Dost eternity enfold,
Endless being, uncontrolled,
Freedom, more than heart can hold,
Every wave a hope divine,
Sun-charms, golden line on line,
Thou great moving mystery-shrine?
Thine the first sounds that the earth
Heard, its cradle-song at birth.
Hidden voices in thy deep
Half untold their secret keep,
As they murmur evermore
Old-world tidings to the shore.
Glorious sea, thy moving light
Spreads round earth a mantle bright,

Wide as range of eye or mind,
Tameless playmate of the wind.
Like a shuttle glancing free
In and out, thy life, O sea,
Whatsoe'er thy mood hath been,
Weaves a web of magic sheen.
Gracious wandering life, the air
Sports around thee for its share;
Winds that move, and winds that rest,
Heaving softly on thy breast,
Like a sea-bird from the crest,
Rise from off thy waves, and fly,
Sweeping fresh the summer sky.
Glorious sea, glad, unconfined,
Free as range of eye or mind,
Tameless playmate of the wind,
Gracious power, whate'er thou be,
Lay thy sweetest liberty
At the pilgrims' feet, O sea.

VI.

THE COLONY.[1]

East and west, and north and south,
As if we were shot from a cannon's mouth,
   Hurrah, hurrah ! here we all are.
  Never was heard in peace or war,
    The first in the world are we,
Never, oh, never, was heard before,
     Since a ball was a ball,
     And a wall a wall,
    And a boy to play was free,
That a school as old as an old oak-tree,
  Fast by the roots, was flung up in the air,
  Up in the air without thought or care,
And pitched on its feet by the sea, the sea,
   Pitched on its feet by the sea.

[1] School Song.

Ere the old school walls were dumb
  With the silence of despair,
"March, boys, march! the end has come!"
  Rang the watchword proud and clear.
We our standard rallied round,
Thrice a hundred faithful found.

Playgrounds—leagues on leagues of shore;
  Class-rooms—all the sea-king's caves;
We are touched by Ariel's power,
  Free of air, and earth, and waves.
We are elves of Ariel's range,
Nought but suffers a sea change.

Ah! the wand has laid its spell
  Over cricket-fields and trees;
Presto!—woods, and mountains, shells,
  Rocks, and sea-anemones;
Thrice turn round and shut your eyes,
Open to a fresh surprise.

Open on the level sward
    Slid Gogerddan's [1] hills between.
When Gogerddan's genial lord
    Looked upon the starry green,
Lady-bright with summer stars,
Heard the schoolboys' loud hurrahs.

Lo! the panting cricket train
    Up the valley slowly creeps,
Lo! a boyish hurricane
    E'en o'er Cader Idris sweeps.
Never in the good greenwood
Lived more gaily Robin Hood.

Little bits of fairy world,
    Fairy streamlets, dropping rills,
And the Lery [2] softly curled
    In amongst the dreaming hills:

---

[1] Gogerddan, the seat of Sir Pryse Pryse, Bart.
[2] The river at Borth.

Never in the good greenwood
Lived more gaily Robin Hood.

East and west, and north and south,
As if we were shot from a cannon's mouth,
   Hurrah, hurrah! here we all are.
  Never was heard in peace or war,
    The first in the world are we,
Never, oh, never, was heard before,
    Since a ball was a ball,
    And a wall a wall,
   And a boy to play was free,
That a school as old as an old oak-tree,
  Fast by the roots, was flung up in the air,
  Up in the air without thought or care,
And pitched on its feet by the sea, the sea,
   Pitched on its feet by the sea.

VII.

RIPPLES.[1]

JOLLY, O, jolly, at eve,
When the golden waves
Are tumbling into the sun,
   And the silent air
Is thinking of nothing, to run
     Down to the shore,
     Boys by the score,
Into the hollow way
Curved by the ebbing spray,
Chasing him back to his watery den,
Lightly, O, lightly he leaps out again.
Backward, O, backward we run
(Thinking-of-nothing-o fun)!
Jolly wet every one.

[1] School Song.

Rare, O, rare,
Nought can compare
When the silent air
Is thinking of nothing, to run,
In thinking-of-nothing-o fun,
Out on the ebbing wave,
Chasing him back to his watery lair,
Jolly wet every one,
Thinking-of-nothing-o fun!

Jolly, O, jolly, at eve,
When the golden waves
Are tumbling into the sun,
   And the silent air
Is thinking of nothing, to go,
     All in a row,
     A hundred or so,
Manfully take a stand,
Just on the edge of the land,

Just where the pebbles and inrushing sea
Battle, and rattle, and never agree,
Solemnly, solemnly, O!
Each his own pebble to throw,
With a heigho! jolly heigho!
Rare, O, rare,
Nought can compare
  When the silent air
Is thinking of nothing, to go,
With a heigho! jolly heigho!
Solemnly, solemnly, throw
Pebbles and pebbles at our jolly foe,
Hundreds of heads in a row,
Thinking of nothing, heigho!

VIII.

THE LERY.[1]

O HAPPY days, O happy days,
    Ye pass, but do not die,
Bright visitants, like summer rain
    Dropped softly from the sky;
Which rests awhile on earth,
And sinks unseen, and reappears again
    In wondrous birth on birth,
New born in herb and flower, in bud and tree,
And fountain waters flowing clear and free.

O happy days, thy glow is on
    Green slope and heathery hill,
Reflection bright of happy eyes,
    Which there have looked their fill.

[1] The river by Borth.

Ye choose ye valleys sweet,
Where o'er the water-song the dim woods rise,
  Your votaries to meet,
And sweetest far your home where Lery bright
Plays in your smile with pebbles and the light.

We find you where we left you last,
  When that glad summer noon
We turned to go, half gay, half sad,
  An end had come so soon;
Just where the wider sweep,
  With oak, and fern, and purple heather clad,
Curves from the shoulder steep,
Whereon ye watch the streamlet down the glade
Send its white thoughts through narrowing glooms of shade.

Look, now th' imprisoned light is spread
    On a clear bed of rock;
And the next moment tossed about,
    A fairy shuttlecock;
    Then in a still pool deep,
Heart laid to heart in chambers hollowed out,
    The quiet wood doth sleep.
So wooing still and wooed, demure or gay,
The Lery down the vale a soul of joy doth stray.

Thy train, dear happy days, are here,
    Each leaflet in its place,
They tell me round yon jutting rock
    That I shall see your face.
    Lo! all are paddling there,
For happy time recks not of mortal clock,
    The children of last year.
Our fishers throw, while on the pebbly ridge
Tea boils, and rash feet shake the miner's bridge.

Each tendril the old welcome gives,
    Each leaflet in its place,
The very ants are marching still
    Along the selfsame trace;
    The hours themselves forget
To drop another shadow on the rill,
    So there it lingers yet,
And year by year we wake up with a kiss
The sleeping princess of our summer bliss.

IX.

THE SANDS.

Each shall have his own love,
    High be linked to high,
Sky be kissing mountain,
    Mountain kissing sky.

Dozing in the orchard
    Let the goodman sit,
Count on summer evenings
    Apples he will eat.

Glory to the sands O!
    Glory give who can,
Where a man, who stands O!
    Feels himself a man.

Where the east wind gallops,
    Keen with keen-edged knife,
And the wide world freshens,
    Salted with sea-life.

Where the great free waters
    Have their freedom rolled,
And the golden sunbeams
    Powdered them with gold.

Blow, ye winds, your trumpets,
    Blow, ye winds, your fife,
Glory to the sands O!
    Salted with sea-life.

With the sea-bird shrieking
    To the sea below,
Clang thy wild clang, sea-bird,
    Sea, thy organ blow.

When the summer whispers
    Float in o'er the sea,
Then a moving rainbow
    Spreads itself o'er thee.

Rainbow light and silver,
    Silver sheen and gold,
All the light of childhood,
    Happy childhood bold.

There it gleams and glistens,
    Moving as we go,
Light of sun or childhood,
    Who is skilled to know?

Liberty and joyance
    Still ye give each one,
Manhood with the east wind,
    Childhood with the sun.

Blow, ye winds, your trumpets,
    Blow, ye winds, your fife,
Glory to the sands O!
    Salted with sea-life.

With the sea-bird shrieking
    To the sea below;
Clang thy wild clang, sea-bird,
    Sea, thy organ blow.

X.

THE MARSH CIRCLE.

CHIMES there are on earth, harmonious splendours,
    Subtle symphonies of ear and eye,
Yea, dim bridals, when the mortal spirit
    Weds a half-veiled immortality.

Moments, as when some dumb, wistful creature
    Gazes in its master's eyes, to find
Deeps on deeps, and wins a higher nature
    By mysterious touch of higher mind.

Whoso sees the deep eyes turned upon him,
    Nature's dreamlike radiance, on the height
Breathless-happy stands, and draws by seeing
    Blissful inspiration, clearer sight.

Go where from his rampart Taliesin [1]
    O'er the beaten gold of the great plain
Throws his charm on river, sea, and mountain,
    Blending all in one bright living strain.

Now a sunny silence makes heart-music,
    As it comes up smiling o'er the sea;
All the hill-sides dimple; on it passes,
    In and out the enchanted shadows flee.

Now within the coronet of mountains
    And the sea-fringed margin of the west
Nature's thoughts are stirring, gusts of passion
    Ruffle the embroidery on her breast.

Far away a trouble on the waters
    'Gins to whiten, then a living veil

---

[1] Taliesin, the great Welsh Bard, buried on a hill overlooking the plain of Borth.

Drops down from the sky, black gleam the head-
    lands,
    Gleam the hills through drifts of shadowy
        trail.

And the weird wild freedom of the marshland
    Stretches, breadths on breadths of level gold,
Where the storm-scuds wander, and the rainbow
    In the midst lets fall its glittering hold.

Broad, bright plain, free wanderland of fancy,
    Robed in colours, all the sun can weave
Out of silver seas, and hill-sides glooming,
    Molten in the ruddy fires of eve,

Cloth of gold from sands, and silken tissue
    Spun from the blue distance, threads of white
Shot through by the rivers, crimson buddings
    Of the oak groves flushed with spring delight.

He on whom the deep eyes once have turned their
    Hidden splendours, be he where he will,
Evermore a prophet's dream enfolding,
    Walks with yearnings which he ne'er can fill.

XI.

SHELLS.

FAIRIES all, whoever ran
Pell-mell from smoke-witted man,
Scared from haunted well and tree
Fairy mermaidens to be,
Colonists of fairy sea;
Empire found, and perils o'er,
Soon ye peeped out on the shore,
Frolic-bold as heretofore;
Village green and woodland spells
Lightly changed for shells O, shells!
Your sea besoms twice a day
(Swish, and swirl, and hissing spray)
Brush all mortal taint away.

Twice a day the saucy waves,
Heads bent low, your merry slaves,
Tumble in of shells a store
From the sea-king's palace floor.
On a day remembered well,
Never butterfly befell
Brighter bursting from his cell,
Picked we the first fairy shell.
Time his hinge had backward swung,
Youth and Age together sprung
In a world where all was young.
Age was young and Youth as old,
Age and Youth, two children bold,
Caught old Time with potent spells,
Magic words of shells O, shells!
Shells—the very air did seem
Opening into some bright dream,
And an unseen gladness swept
All around us as we stept.

Miles of hope before us lay,
Golden, glistening sheets of day,
With a sea-charm washed alway;
Fairy-sprinkled! who could tell?
Every yard might give its shell;
Little Cockles' pearly sheen,
Chariot fit for fairy queen,
Pectens, dipped in colours won
From the rays slipped off the sun
In the waves, when day is done.
Here a ripple in and out
Mocking whirls the Cones about,
Brings them to our fingers, then
Laughs, and swings them off again.
There a dark line softly lies
Rich in promise 'neath the skies;
Happy he foredoomed to burst
On that fairy treasure first,
Ere assailed by foot accurst,

Of the jealous, tricksy sea
Rushing catch him to the knee,
And with slow malicious glee
Gently suck it back; ah me!
Shells O, shells! the slanted hail,
Thunder-driven, blind, and pale,
Beat on rovers bent, subdued,
Each apart in solitude,
Nursing his own woeful mood.
Lo! a shell bank—at the cry
Sunshine flashed along the sky,
Reckless-bright each sunny eye
Glistened, on the spoil they fly,
Cockles, Mactras, Artemis,
Pectens, unknown shapes of bliss,
Turritella, Tellens frail,
Orphans, delicate and pale,
Newly risen from the sea
Peerless Venus Chione.

Such a ring was never seen
Glancing coy on minstrel's een
In the sweetest, shyest gloom
Of the young world's maiden bloom,
Ere the tender dew had died
Hopeless, on the mountain-side,
And away the fairies hied.
Where the fairies hied would'st know
To the printless margin go,
Where sea besoms twice a day
(Swish, and swirl, and hissing spray)
Purge all mortal taint away,
There the fairy children play.

XII.

SUNDAY.—THE HILL-TOP.

How softly leading upward, the green slope
   Leans 'gainst the southern sky,
And restful feet have reached the top before
   They know they are so high.

E'en so, up from the levels of the week,
   In its own quiet air,
Enthroned within a more ethereal blue,
   The Sunday rises fair.

And ofttimes, as God's peace from church and
      field
   Upon their spirit lay,
A happy group down set made all their own
   That gracious place and day.

Far down the shadowy tracts of gleaming sand
    Seemed melting from the eye,
And all the busy week, a few dark specks,
    Which sight could scarce descry.

The small waves chattered all along the shore;
    But with low pleading sweet
The billows crept up to the tall black rocks,
    And clasped their giant feet.

And there in talk, or silence dearer still,
    They let their hearts go free,
In that sweet confidence, which nothing asks
    But being still to be.

The sea discourses to them, or they launch
    On summer clouds, that throw
A purple mantle wrought in peaceful skies
    On dreaming waves below.

And gathering up the light of the great plain,
    A web of colours rare,
They blend them, as they look, with fancies meet,
    And peace of upper air,

Till where the river 'twixt the distant hills
    Leads up into the skies,
In that fair borderland of earth and heaven
    The changeful glory lies.

Whoso within that dreamy circle sits,
    For him abideth still
The calm of upper air, the magic light
    That hill sends on to hill.

XIII.

THE RETURN.[1]

Salt, and sand, and rocking wave,
    Salt, and sand, and sky,
All ye had to give ye gave,
    But—good-bye, good-bye.
Hey, the robin, the lark, and the green green grass,
And the ivy that clings to the wall;
Hey, the robin, the lark, and the green green grass,
And the oak, and the ash-tree tall.

Rocking wave, and mountain bold,
    Bright air, free to roam,

[1] School Song.

Say not that our hearts are cold;
Oh! but—home is home.
Hey, the robin, the lark, and the green green grass,
And the ivy that clings to the wall;
Hey, the robin, the lark, and the green green grass,
And the oak, and the ash-tree tall.

Smoothest turf, a sunshine floor,
Dance of cricket ball,
Studies, where we shut the door
On our cosy all.
Hey, the robin, the lark, and the green green grass,
And the ivy that clings to the wall;
Hey, the robin, the lark, and the green green grass,
And the oak, and the ash-tree tall.

Grey old school-house, consecrate
　　On thy hill afar,
Chapel, keeping solemn state—
　　Home we go, hurrah !
Hey, the robin, the lark, and the green green grass,
And the ivy that clings to the wall ;
Hey, the robin, the lark, and the green green grass,
And the oak, and the ash-tree tall.

XIV.

THE FLAGS.[1]

To him, who wounded turned aside,
It mattered little that he died
In sunshine, in the fair springtide.

On many a grave the flowers are gay,
Oft ruin creeping on his prey
Puts forth a velvet paw in play.

O Flags, ye wrap within your fold
A stranger tale than e'er was told
Of Muses' sons in days of old.

[1] School Song.

The homeless school, of fortune braved,
Will aye remember how ye waved
Above them, in the hour that saved.

As long as youth breathes living fire,
As long as scorn is on the liar,
And men can mount from high to higher.

Rest in the school-room, rest, and be
A spirit moving calm and free,
A silent flame of liberty.

Say, peace more stern than war demands
Devotion purer, cleaner hands,
Life larger, foot that firmer stands.

Bid Hope his thrilling clarion blow,
And fearless truth in boyhood glow,
And honour send him on his foe.

So life shall foster life, each son
Still better what his sire hath done,
And truth from truth full circle run.

www.ingramcontent.com/pod-product-compliance
Lightning Source LLC
Chambersburg PA
CBHW022149090426
42742CB00010B/1434